THE SCHOLARLY BANANA

PRESENTS

FITCHER'S BIRD

A CLASSIC FAIRY TALE FROM THE BROTHERS GRIMM

The Scholarly Banana Presents Fitcher's Bird:
A Classic Fairy Tale from the Brothers Grimm

Copyright © 2019 Karly West
www.thescholarlybanana.com

All rights reserved. This book or any portion thereof
may not be reproduced or used in any manner whatsoever
without the express written permission of the publisher
except for the use of brief quotations in a book review.

ISBN: 978-1-7338509-1-9
No bananas were harmed in the making of this book.

THE SCHOLARLY CONTENTS

PART ONE: THE INTROS

The part with the *ABOUTS*. About The Scholarly Banana, about the Grimm Brothers, and about Fitcher's Bird.

PART TWO: THE STORY

It's the main event: A summary of Fitcher's Bird, a classic fairy tale from the Brothers Grimm.

PART THREE: THE SCHOLARLY PART

Tales from around the world! A history of serial killers! Symbolism and analysis that will traumatize the bejeezus out of you!

PART FOUR: THE OUTROS

Scholarly references, acknowledgements, and a few more *ABOUTS* for symmetry's sake.

PART ONE
THE INTROS

An attempt to answer humanity's most intriguing questions such as...

WHAT ON EARTH IS THE SCHOLARLY BANANA?

WHO WERE THE GRIMM BROTHERS?

WHAT THE HECK IS FITCHER'S BIRD ABOUT, ANYWAY?*

*SPOILER ALERT: IT'S NOT ABOUT BIRDS

WHAT ON EARTH IS THE SCHOLARLY BANANA?

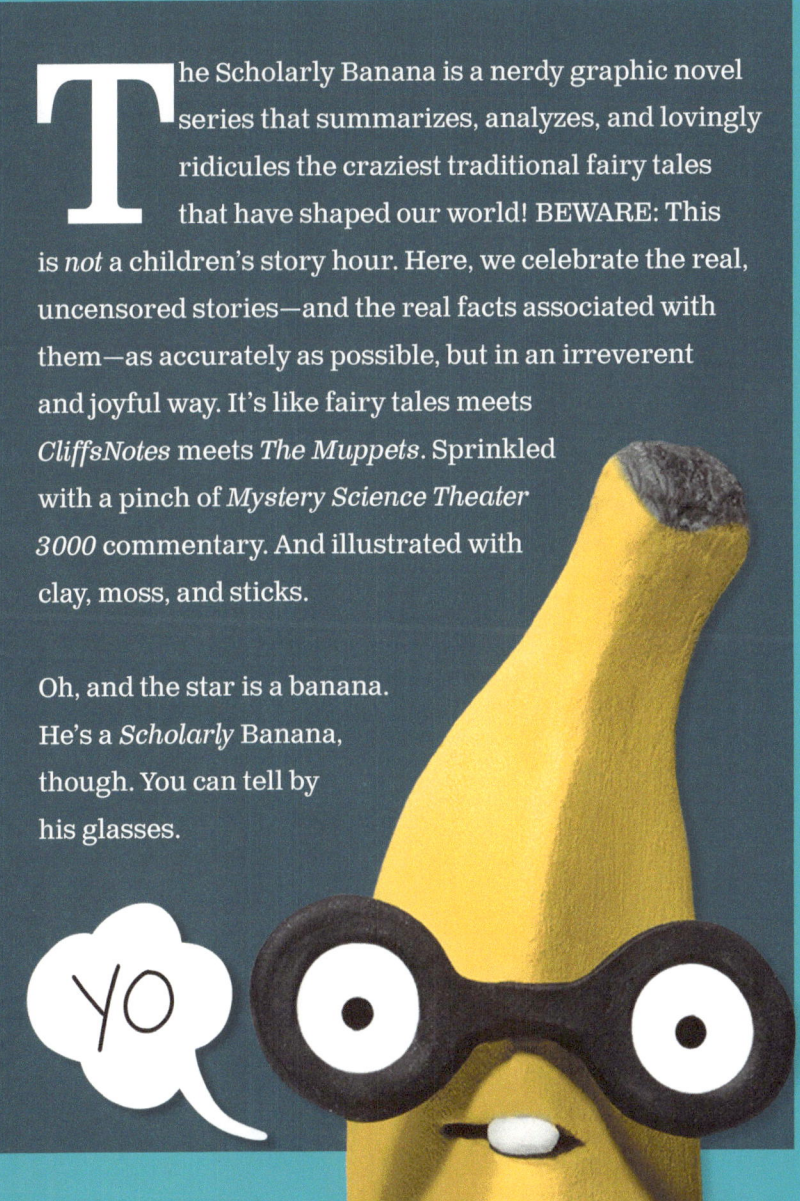

The Scholarly Banana is a nerdy graphic novel series that summarizes, analyzes, and lovingly ridicules the craziest traditional fairy tales that have shaped our world! BEWARE: This is *not* a children's story hour. Here, we celebrate the real, uncensored stories—and the real facts associated with them—as accurately as possible, but in an irreverent and joyful way. It's like fairy tales meets *CliffsNotes* meets *The Muppets*. Sprinkled with a pinch of *Mystery Science Theater 3000* commentary. And illustrated with clay, moss, and sticks.

Oh, and the star is a banana. He's a *Scholarly* Banana, though. You can tell by his glasses.

WHO WERE THE GRIMM BROTHERS?

Once upon a time (the 1800's) in a magical land far away (in a country we now call Germany), there lived two scholarly brothers named Jacob and Wilhelm Grimm. The Grimms were on an academic and patriotic mission: to preserve and celebrate their German culture by bringing their people together through storytelling!

1.) JACOB GRIMM   2.) WILHELM GRIMM   3.) BANANA (NOT A GRIMM)

To accomplish this scholarly feat, the Grimms interviewed local storytellers and transcribed hundreds of old, oral folk tales which were in danger of being forgotten. They published—and in doing so, preserved—these traditional German stories in a book called *Kinder- und Haüsmarchen* (abbreviated as KHM and translated as *Children's Stories and Household Tales*). The Grimms released seven editions of KHM between 1812 and 1857.

Even though the Grimms created KHM to celebrate their *German* heritage, many of their stories were heavily inspired by older *French* fairy tales (Fitcher's Bird is one of these tales.) This makes sense, though! During this time, Germany was not an official country and was under French occupation by Napoleon (hence the Grimms' patriotic mission!) But regardless of their mixed cultural origins, the stories of KHM all exude an unmistakably German (and Grimm) flavor. And they have entertained, enchanted, and horrified us for centuries!

Sacré bleu!

But KHM wasn't always so popular. Ironically, the first edition of *Children's Stories and Household Tales* was not meant for children. Or for normal human beings, for that matter! Originally, KHM was created to be a scholarly research project, not a bestselling book. The stories were raw and uncensored. The tone was academic. And judging by the reviews, the general public was not impressed:

> **"PATHETIC! TASTELESS! KEEP AWAY FROM CHILDREN!"**

While they were both accomplished, hard-working professionals, the Grimms weren't rich. Since book sales were important, the brothers began to rework their "tasteless" stories to appeal to average German families and children. Clearly, this marketing strategy worked! The Grimms continued to rewrite and expand their collection over seven editions and 40 years.

FUN FACT: Of the two brothers, Wilhelm was KHM's editorial powerhouse and a notorious censorship freak. Wilhelm was a real stickler about sexual innuendos. He removed every single one from the later editions of KHM. However, the violence didn't bother him. In fact, he added more!

family fun for all!

Today, KHM's legacy is anything but "pathetic." The Grimms' fairy tale collection is not only one of the most important cultural icons of Germany, but the entire western world! And here's a fun fact: According to *The Annotated Brothers Grimm*, KHM is the 3rd best-selling book of all time, ranking after the Bible and the works of Shakespeare! Clearly, these stories mean a lot to us. Or maybe we're under a spell.

WHAT THE HECK IS FITCHER'S BIRD ABOUT, ANYWAY?

Glad you asked! Fitcher's Bird was largely inspired by Bluebeard, a French fairy tale written by Charles Perrault about one hundred years earlier (1697). While these two fairy tales aren't very well-known today, (for reasons we'll get into later) you're probably more familiar with them than you think! In many ways, they're similar to Beauty and the Beast! The big difference is that in Bluebeard and Fitcher's Bird, "the beast" is not a handsome, enchanted prince. He's a mangy, rabid beast. Who kills people...And keeps corpses in the house.

AND LOOKS LIKE THIS GUY.
Bluebeard Illustration by Gustave Doré (1862)

★ ★ ★ ★ ★

"IF YOU'RE INTO GIANT BIRD-PEOPLE YOU'LL PROBABLY LOVE IT! "

Fitcher's Bird is one of the grimmest of the Grimm tales. So if you're into evil wizards, brutal murders, bloody basins, and giant bird-people (hey, I'm not judging), you'll probably love it! Alas, I don't think *The Cartoon Mouse* will be appropriating this story any time soon. So for now, a Scholarly Banana will have to do. Alrighty, then! Let's get to it!

PART TWO
THE STORY

Presenting Fitcher's Bird,
a classic fairy tale from the Brothers Grimm.

······· **STARRING** ·······

THE SCHOLARLY BANANA

as Fitcher

······· **ALSO WITH** ·······

Girl #1

Girl #2

Girl #3

The Village People

The Mob

FITCHER'S BIRD

ONCE UPON A TIME, THERE LIVED A SEXUAL PREDATOR NAMED FITCHER.

Our lead villain, Fitcher, has an impressive resume of evilness. Not only is he a serial kidnapper and a notorious creep, but he happens to be a magical wizard too. As you can imagine, Fitcher's particular brand of wizardry keeps the nearby town in a constant amber alert.

Fitcher's favorite pastime is what I like to call *recreational begging*. That is, he loves to cosplay as a hungry beggar, wander around town, and hunt for unsuspecting victims. Whenever a kind-hearted girl offers him charity or a scrap of food, Fitcher shows his appreciation by forcibly abducting her in a magical basket. He then totes her away to god-knows-where, never to be seen again. Needless to say, the townsfolk are not amused by this.

One lovely day, Fitcher goes a-creeping to a house where three beautiful daughters reside. He performs his signature basket trick on the oldest girl and whisks her away to a secondary crime scene, also known as his *dark forest lair*.

You should know that, technically, Fitcher's lair isn't so much a lair as it is a pimped-out palace of awesomeness. Being a professional wizard must be a lucrative gig because Fitcher's lair has entire rooms filled with gold and jewels!

Despite his evil nature and general skeeziness, Fitcher seems to be a fabulous entertainer as well as a gracious host. *That is, as far as wizard-perverts are concerned. I'm grading him on a curve.* You see, Fitcher genuinely wants his victim to be happy living in forced captivity with him. And believe it or not, it sounds like she was! The girl doesn't seem to care that Fitcher just stole her off the front stoop. Perhaps the gold and jewels are throwing her off.

REVIEWS

THE_FIRSTGIRL_1812
AMAAAZING!!

OMG YOU GUYS! This is literally the BEST. LAIR. EVER. The wizard guy is a little evil so that's why I'm deducting a star. But there is literally so much gold. The basket ride was a little cramped, but otherwise it's MAGICAL!!! ;)

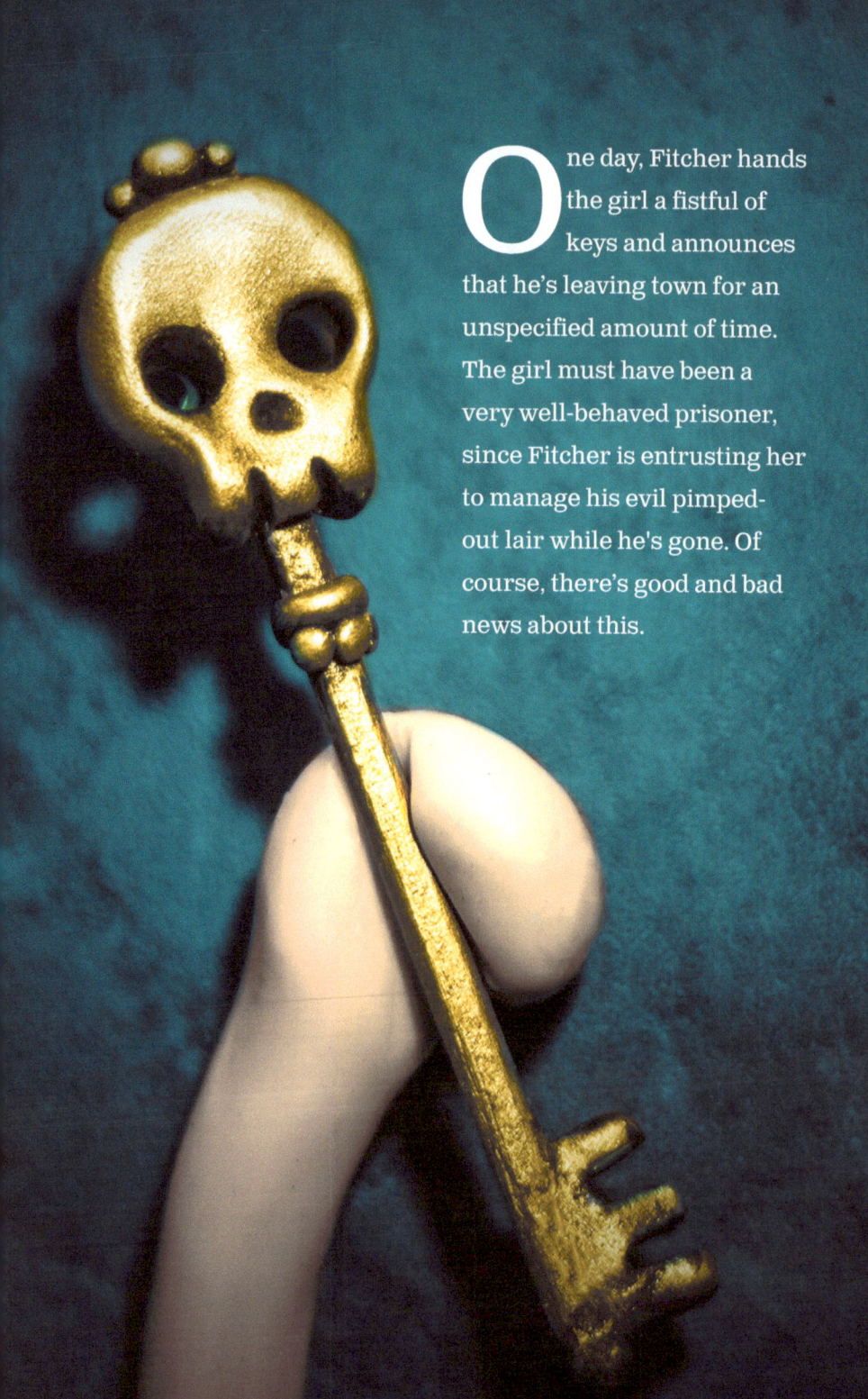

One day, Fitcher hands the girl a fistful of keys and announces that he's leaving town for an unspecified amount of time. The girl must have been a very well-behaved prisoner, since Fitcher is entrusting her to manage his evil pimped-out lair while he's gone. Of course, there's good and bad news about this.

THE GOOD NEWS

The girl is free to explore Fitcher's entire lair while he's gone!

THE FREAKISHLY TERRIBLE NEWS

If she enters the aforementioned forbidden room, Fitcher will straight-up murder her.

Then Fitcher hands the girl an egg, mostly because this story wants to be as weird as possible. He says she must carry it everywhere. At all times. For no particular reason. Fitcher warns her that if this random egg gets lost, he'll be really ticked off.

Remember, Fitcher's lair has entire rooms filled with gold and jewels. You'd think that he'd have an "egg room" if it were really that important. Or a safe. Or a carton. But I digress.

After laying down the house rules/death threats, Fitcher leaves and the girl starts exploring. At first, she seems to be the perfect model of trustworthiness by carefully obeying all of Fitcher's (rather asinine) instructions about the egg. But alas, she doesn't take Fitcher's warnings about the *Forbidden Room of Death* quite as seriously. In fact, she goes straight for it. With egg in hand.

Unlike the dazzling gold and jewel-filled rooms, Fitcher's forbidden man-cave is clearly the private, functional space of his home. Its style is bold and masculine, like a cross between *Jigsaw* Revival and *Hostel* Chic. Accordingly, Fitcher has furnished it simply with an antique wood block, a gleaming ax, and a basin full of blood.

Apparently, Fitcher and the girl have very different tastes in interior design. In fact, the girl is so shocked by Fitcher's ugly man-cave that she accidentally hurls the egg right into the blood basin. Oopsies.

OH fudge

So, the girl didn't see this coming, eh? This raises an interesting question, namely: What *did* she expect to find inside a murderous wizard's "forbidden room?" The underground railroad? Canned goods for the homeless? Foster puppy shelter? Your guess is as good as mine. It's a mystery wrapped in a riddle inside a basin of blood. Also, I'm no doctor, but in my professional medical opinion, the gold and jewels have caused serious damage to this girl's brain.

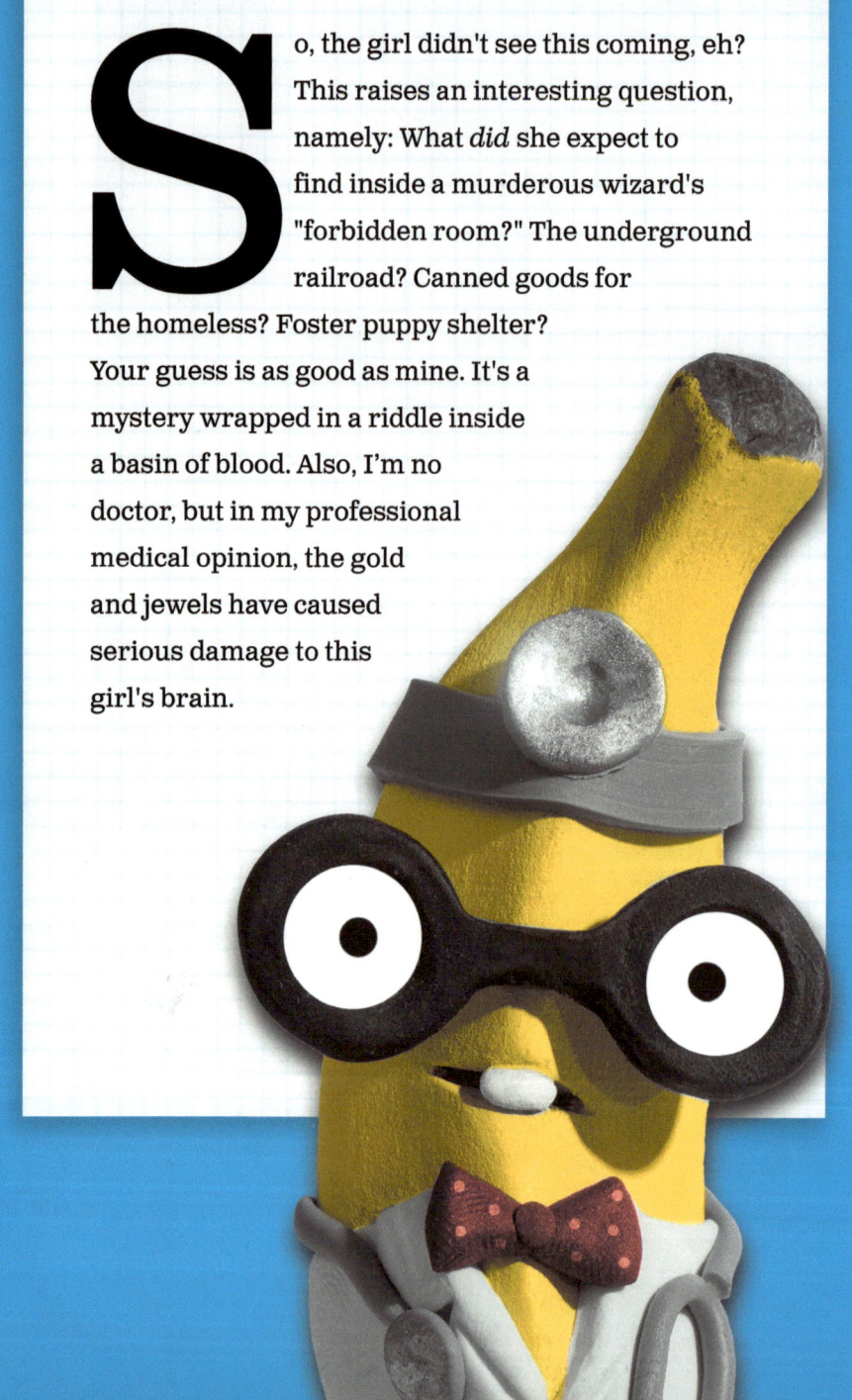

Mental issues aside, the girl manages to fish the egg out of the basin *Double Dare* style. But alas, Fitcher's precious random egg is now dyed with blood. It's like the worst Easter ever.

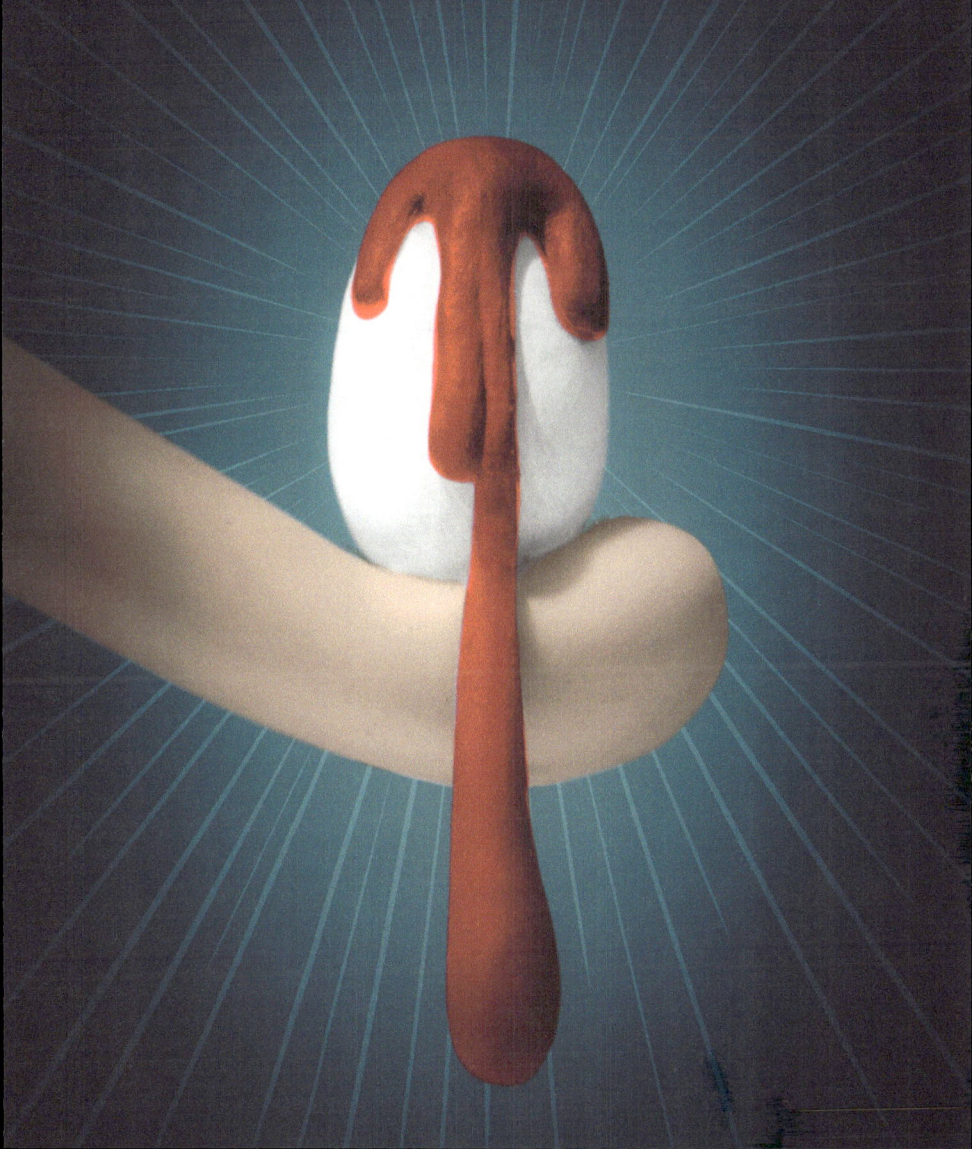

"There HAS to be a better WAY!!!"

Everyone knows that blood stains are super tricky to get out. The girl wipes, scrubs and scours the egg, but nothing is working. The stain-fighting power of *OxiClean* may have helped, but unfortunately, this story takes place about 100 years before Billy Mays was invented.

Now guess who suddenly reappears at this critical and horrible moment. Yep, our friend Fitcher has unexpectedly returned! Right on cue.

Fitcher greets the girl.
He sees the bloody egg.
And as promised...

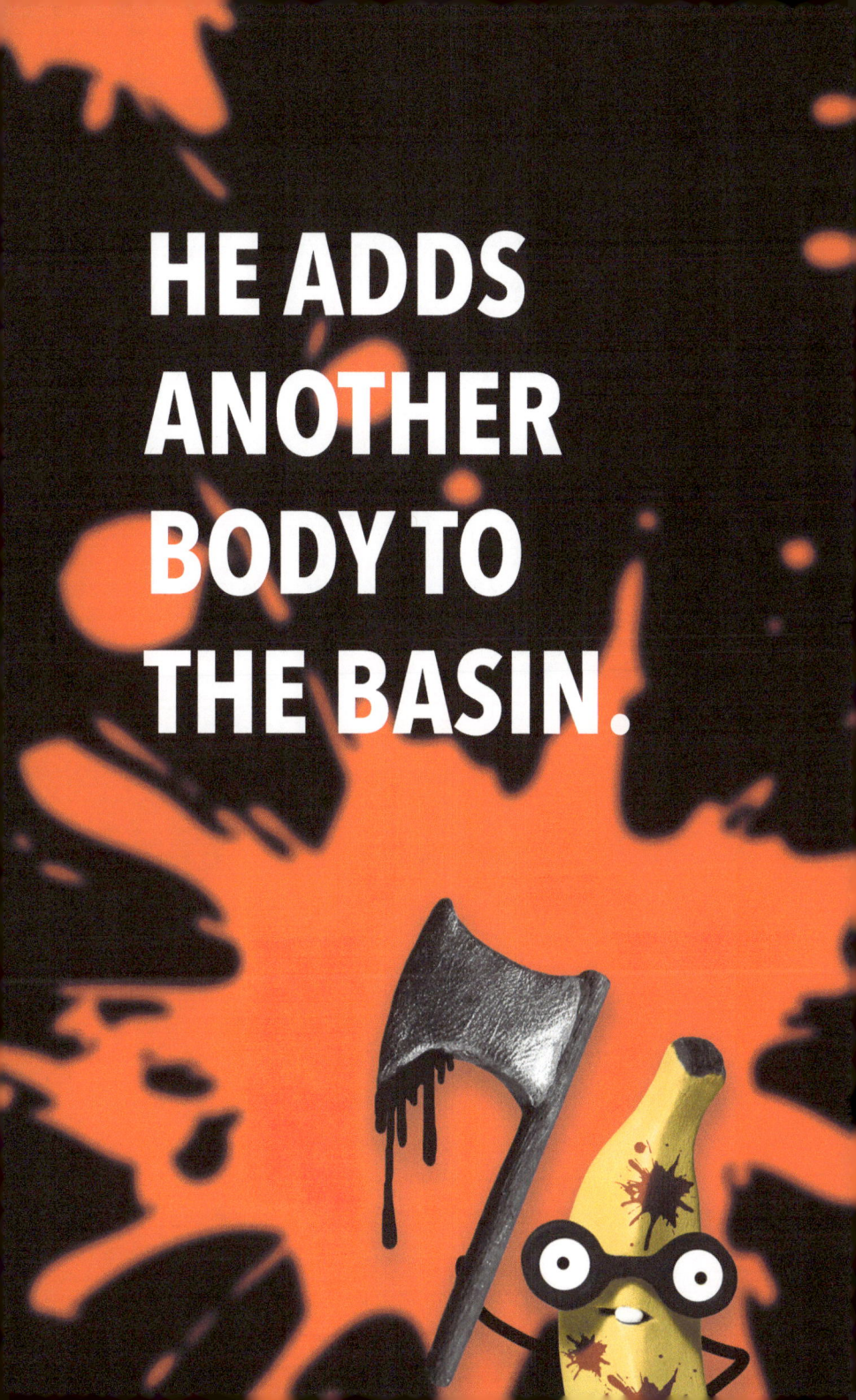

THE EXACT SAME EVENTS REPEAT IN THE EXACT SAME WAY.

After the second homicide is complete, Fitcher returns to the village to shop for his third and final victim. Naturally, he returns to the exact same house to do this.

> It's a very up-and-coming neighborhood

BANANA Realty — PRICE REDUCED

I don't know about you but if I were this poor family, I definitely would've moved by now.

As per usual, Fitcher leaves his newest victim with his key, his egg, and his standard-issue death threats. But since fairy tales have a thing for doing things in threes, this time there's a twist! Unlike the first two fools, the third girl is crafty and sly (Fairy Tale Translation: she knows that schlepping a random egg around for no reason is dumb). So as soon as Fitcher leaves, she promptly ditches it. Then the third girl heads straight to the forbidden room, unencumbered by the slippery egg of death.

Of course, when Girl #3 enters the forbidden room, she discovers the blood basin, which, unfortunately, is overflowing with her dismembered kin. So that's kind of a bummer.

But never fear! Death is negotiable in fairy tales if it serves the plot. The crafty girl aligns the bloody stumps, smushes them together like a jigsaw puzzle, and by the power of fantasy fiction...

Curiously, instead of fleeing for their lives, shouting for help, or arming themselves with axes, the three sisters decide to hang around the crime scene and relax for a while. The third girl/necromancer hides her freshly-reanimated sisters somewhere in the house. Then everyone just mulls around and waits for Fitcher—the ax-wielding psychopath—to come back. And speaking of whom...

Fitcher busts back onto the scene in his signature calculated and oh-so-creepy way. He greets the girl like always, but this time he sees that his precious egg is *egg-colored*! There isn't even a speck of blood on it! And with that, Fitcher declares that Girl #3 has passed the test. She has won! Oh, happy day!

AND HER PRIZE?

Why it's a marriage with
FITCHER HIMSELF!

Alrighty then. As her first order of wedding business, the girl tells Fitcher to deliver a basket of gold to her parents' house. He must carry it on his back and must never stop to rest. She warns him that she'll be watching from the attic window to make sure he doesn't slack off.

Even wizards are powerless against a Bridezilla's wrath, so Fitcher doesn't argue with her. Nor does he question the limits of human eyesight.

I still see you

Meanwhile, the two sisters are hiding inside the basket, hitching a free ride home. Apparently, mule-ing around a basket of gold (plus two stowaways) is grueling work, even for wizards. But every time Fitcher slows down, one of the sisters harps at him to keep moving. Naturally, Fitcher assumes that the nagging voice (which is coming from directly behind his ear) is his fiancée (who is god-knows-how-many-miles away). So he dutifully plods along.

Back at Fitcher's lair, the third girl is busy making handmade crafts for the wedding. She finds a skull (presumably there are lots of them laying around) and bedazzles it with flowers and jewels. Then she proudly displays the decorated human remains in the attic window, facing the road. Note: This is what brides did before Pinterest. It was her best idea.

The Dreamiest Wedding Trends of 1812

13 Wedding Ideas To Try

Corpse Decoration in 43 Easy Steps

DIY Wedding Skull

bin it

binterest

Then the girl slathers herself with honey, rips open a mattress, and rolls around in a heap of feathers until she resembles a giant sticky chicken. Now that she's feeling fly, the third girl heads towards town looking like a cross between a mental patient and a Muppet.

Our feather-encrusted friend encounters a group of travelers on the road. In a stroke of extreme fairy tale-like coincidence, these characters are her invited wedding guests heading to Fitcher's lair to celebrate the romantic occasion. Let's hope they kept their gift receipts.

Although the story is vague about time lines, it feels like Fitcher's "engagement" just happened! How does everyone know about this? Sounds like news travels crazy-fast in this quaint little fairy tale village. Maybe the Bird Girl *tweeted* it?

TheThirdGirl ✓ @TheThirdGirl

OMG got engaged to @fitcherwizard Hes evil AF. Somebody save me! THX!!!

Now that we've gotten to know the village people, let's see how their bizarre conversations with Bird Girl went down. NOTE: The conversation you're about to read is a quote. The pictures have been changed to protect the innocent.

You probably noticed that during these conversations, no one asks how a bird managed to sprout human legs, why it reeks of honey, or if this is some kind of bizarre performance art. In fact, the villagers seem to believe that this sticky feathered refugee is a real, legit bird. I'll admit, natural science was never my best subject so I'll just go with it.

CREATURES OF THE WORLD
ACCORDING TO FITCHER'S BIRD

FIG. 1   FIG. 2   FIG. 3

1. HUMAN (HOMO SAPIENS)   **2. BIRD (AVES)**   **3. BANANA (MUSA ACUMINATA)**

Further down the road, the girl bumps into Fitcher himself, who is now on his way home from gold delivery. And wouldn't you know it—they have that exact same conversation too. Rhymes and all.

I must say, this girl must be one heck of a costume designer! Even Fitcher—her own husband/captor—doesn't recognize her. Just like the others, Fitcher thinks she's a real bird. Naturally, he doesn't ask questions about this extremely-questionable situation.

"Hey girl!... I'm coming HOME!"

Instead, he smiles and waves at the inanimate skull that's propped up in his attic window. Typical Fitcher.

Eventually, the valiant Fitcher returns home. Only mildly exhausted from his human trafficking duties, he's ready for his fairy tale wedding and tonight he's gonna party like it's 1799! As he approaches his lair, Fitcher is glad to see that many wedding guests have already arrived. However, he's slightly *less-glad* to see that a vengeful mob is lurking there too...

The vengeful mob has come to rescue Girl #3 who, for all we know, is still wandering around the village somewhere. Encrusted in honey and feathers. And probably bees.

In lieu of a typical wedding present, the vengeful mob bestows upon Fitcher the gift of *righteous justice*. In other words, they trap him inside his evil lair and burn it to the ground.

AND THUS OUR STORY ENDS. FITCHER DIES A PAINFUL, FIREY DEATH.

THE END

PART THREE
THE SCHOLARLY PART

A discussion of scholarly matters about Fitcher's Bird, including its history, comparative literature, and phallic symbols.

SIMILAR TALES FROM AROUND THE WORLD

HISTORICAL FIGURES WHO MAY HAVE INSPIRED THIS STORY

SYMBOLISM & OVER ANALYSIS

SIMILAR
FAIRY TALES
FROM AROUND THE WORLD

If you love stories about murderous husbands, forbidden chambers, and blood basins, you're in luck my mentally-warped friend! Here's a list of seven traditional fairy tales similar to Fitcher's Bird. I'm sure that these classic *husband-as-monster* stories will satisfy your inner fairy tale nerd. Or in this case, your inner blood lust. Enjoy!

INDIA
THE BRAHMAN GIRL WHO MARRIED A TIGER

The antagonist in this story is not an evil wizard—he's a smooth-talking, shape-shifting tiger!

GERMANY
THE HARE

Meanwhile, the villain in this older German tale is a naughty garden rabbit.

ITALY

HOW THE DEVIL
MARRIED 3 SISTERS

The Italian version goes straight to the point by casting Satan himself as the bad guy! And his forbidden room? It's a portal to Hell!

PALESTINE
ZERENDAC

Sometimes, even Satan isn't extreme enough! This villain from Palestine is a magical monster who challenges his wives in the most wonderfully bizarre way: He asks them to eat his ears, which he deli-slices fresh from his magical monster head.

GERMANY
THE ROBBER BRIDEGROOM

The Robber Bridegroom is another great story from the Grimm Brothers. It teaches essential survival skills like how to navigate the perilous German wilderness using just your courage, your wits, and pocketful of lentils!

ENGLAND

MR. FOX

This fairy tale from Joseph Jacobs is the English version of *The Robber Bridegroom*. Contrary to what the title suggests, there are no foxes in this story. However, it *does* offer inspirational (albeit contradictory) life advice about being bold.

FRANCE
BLUEBEARD

According to Charles Perrault's *Bluebeard,* we don't need wits, boldness, or even lentils, for that matter! All we need to escape a deranged, scimitar-wielding husband is a good, old-fashioned *deus ex machina* (that is, a few capable brothers) to randomly appear and rescue us from our own stupidity and poor life choices. In the absolute knick of time.

These stories are in the public domain, so go forth and read them if you're feeling bold (but not too bold). Just remember to scatter lentils on the path, put the egg in a safe place, eat the ears, and if all else fails, just wait for a random brother to save you.

CREEPY
HISTORICAL FIGURES
WHO MAY HAVE INSPIRED FITCHER'S BIRD

GILLES DE RAIS

Gilles de Rais (1404-1446) was a powerful French nobleman and decorated war hero who fought alongside Joan of Arc. But alas, he's not as famous for his bravery as he is for being a deranged satanist who abused and murdered hundreds of children. Researchers believe that De Rais could be the real-life inspiration for *Bluebeard*—the older, French-er version of *Fitcher's Bird*.

FUN FACT: De Rais is often considered to be history's first serial killer.

THE LEGEND OF CUNMAR THE CURSED

Cunmar the Cursed (ad 500) was an ancient Breton chieftain who had a nasty habit of killing his pregnant wives. Things were going well for Cunmar until Tryphine, his newly-pregnant 5th wife, discovered her husband's dirty little secret. And she promptly ran away.

Unfortunately for Tryphine, she didn't run fast enough. Cunmar caught and decapitated her on the road. However, things started looking up for Tryphine when a man named St. Gildas found her and miraculously cured her detached head. Thus Tryphine and her unborn son were saved and were eventually canonized as saints. While Cunmar didn't achieve *saint status* himself (the murders may have disqualified him), his brutal legend has lived on through equally brutal fairy tales like Bluebeard and Fitcher's Bird. So thanks, Cunmar.

SYMBOLS & ANALYSIS

WHICH WILL PROBABLY RUIN THE STORY FOR YOU AND WILL SURELY TRAUMATIZE YOUR INNER CHILD FOREVER. YOU HAVE BEEN WARNED.

But what does it all mean?

THE EGG

According to psychoanalysts, Fitcher's egg is a symbol of life and female sexuality. In Freudian terms, the staining of the egg—in all its bloody, irreversible glory—represents the loss of the girls' virginity. In other words, Fitcher's random egg isn't random. It's just weird.

You're welcome! And enjoy your breakfast!

THE FORBIDDEN ROOM

Entering the forbidden room isn't just about being a bad house guest. According to researchers, this betrayal symbolizes the girls' sexual infidelity to Fitcher (which seems slightly odd considering the circumstances, but whatever!) As crazy as this interpretation may sound, it's actually based upon a disturbing historical fact: In some parts of the world, a wife's infidelity was a serious crime that was punishable by death. Just like in Fitcher's Bird, if the woman was found guilty, her execution could be administered by her husband. Legally.

THE KEY

Traumatized yet? Well, try to repress your feelings; we've got more over-analyzing to do! Speaking of which, did you know that Fitcher's key isn't a key? Nope, according to Freudian interpretation, the key is a phallic symbol. I'll leave the rest to your imagination.

THE WIZARD

Is it just me, or do you find Fitcher's "wizardry" skills to be a bit lacking? Yes, he does have a magic basket, but let's be real—that's the fairy tale equivalent of driving a creepy white van. So why does the story call Fitcher a "wizard" if he's just an average, murderous fool?

Believe it or not, scholars have a legitimate answer to this ridiculous question! *The Annotated Brothers Grimm* suggests that Fitcher's wizardry is a metaphor for his sexual magnetism demonstrated by his ability to attract his victims in an invisible, unexplainable (and therefore, magical) sort of way.

In other words, according to researchers... Fitcher is sexy?

SEXY

HEY RESEARCHERS, I'M NOT HERE TO JUDGE

Fitcher's Bird Illustration by Arthur Rackham (1917)

THE VERY SPECIAL
BONUS PART

If you've never read Fitcher's Bird before, you may be wondering if the original Grimms' version is as crazy as I made it sound. Well, here it is in all its feather-encrusted glory! The following version of Fitcher's Bird is from the Grimm Brothers' first edition of *Children's Stories and Household Tales* (1812) and was translated by D.L. Ashliman (1999).

FITCHER'S BIRD
THE BANANA-FREE VERSION

Once upon a time there was a sorcerer who was a thief. He disguised himself as a poor man and went begging from house to house. A girl came to the door and brought him a piece of bread. He touched her, and she was forced to jump into his pack basket. Then he carried her to his house where everything was splendid, and he gave her everything that she wanted.

One day he said, "I have to take care of something away from home. I will be away for a while. Here is an egg. Take good care of it. Carry it with you at all times. And here is a key, but at the risk of your life, do not go into the room that it opens. But as soon as he had gone, she unlocked the door and went into the room. In the middle there was a large basin. In it there were dead and dismembered people. She was so terrified that she dropped the egg, which she was holding in her hand, into the basin. She quickly took it out again and wiped off the blood, but it reappeared in an instant. She could not get the egg clean, no matter how much she wiped and scrubbed.

When the man returned, he asked for the egg and the key. He looked at them and knew that she had been in the blood chamber. "You did not heed my words," he said angrily, "and now you are going into the chamber against your will." With that he seized her, led her into the room, cut her up in pieces, and threw her into the basin with the others.

Sometime later the man went begging again. He captured the second daughter from the house, and the same thing happened to her as to the first one. She too opened the forbidden door, dropped the egg into the blood, and was cut to pieces and thrown into the basin.

Then the sorcerer wanted to have the third daughter. He captured her in his pack basket, carried her home, and at his departure gave her the egg and the key. However, the third sister was clever and sly. First of all, she put the egg in a safe place, and then she went into the secret chamber. When she saw her sisters in the basin, she found all of their parts and put each one back in

its right place: head, body, arm, and leg. The parts started to move, and then they joined together, and the two sister came back to life. She took them both out of the room and hid them.

When the man returned and found that the egg was free of blood, he asked her to become his bride. She said yes, but told him that first he would have to carry a basket filled with gold on his back to her parents, and that meanwhile she would be getting ready for the wedding. Then she told her sisters to get help from home. She put them into the basket and covered them over with gold. Then she said to the man, "Carry this away. And don't you dare stop to rest. If you do, I'll be able to see through my window." He lifted the basket onto his back and started off, but it was so heavy that the weight nearly killed him. He wanted to rest a little, but one of the girls inside the basket called out, "I can see through my window that you are resting. Walk on at once!" He thought it was his bride calling out, so he got up and walked on. Every time he wanted to rest, he heard the call, and had to continue on.

Meanwhile, back at his house, his bride dressed up a skull and placed it in the attic window. Then she invited all the sorcerer's friends to the wedding. Then she dipped herself in a barrel of honey, cut open the bed, and rolled in the feathers so that no one would be able to recognize her. In this strange disguise, she left the house and started down the path.

Soon she met some of the guests, who said, "You, Fitcher's bird, where are you coming from?"
"I'm coming from Fitcher's house."
"And what is his young bride doing?"
"She's cleaning the house from bottom to top. Right now she is looking out of the attic window."

Then she also met the bridegroom, who was returning home. "You, Fitcher's bird, where are you coming from?"
"I'm coming from Fitcher's house."
"And what is my young bride doing?"
"She's cleaning the house from bottom to top. Right now she is looking out of the attic window."

The bridegroom looked up, and saw the disguised skull. Thinking it was his bride, he waved to it. But after he arrived home, and all his friends were there as well, the help came that the sisters had sent. They closed up the house and set it afire, and because no one could get out, they all perished in the flames.

SOURCE
Jacob and Wilhelm Grimm, "Fitchers Vogel," Kinder- und Hausmärchen, 1st ed., vol. 1 (Berlin: Realschulbuchhandlung, 1812), no. 46, pp. 200-203. Translated by D. L. Ashliman. © 1999.

PART FOUR
THE OUTROS

A graceful attempt to wrap up this not-so-graceful book.

THE SCHOLARLY RESOURCES

ABOUT THE AUTHOR
ABOUT THE ART

THE SCHOLARLY SHOUT-OUTS

THE SCHOLARLY RESOURCES

THE CLASSIC FAIRY TALES
MARIA TATAR

THE USES OF ENCHANTMENT:
THE MEANING AND IMPORTANCE OF FAIRY TALES
BRUNO BETTELHEIM

THE CLASSIC FAIRY TALES
IONA AND PETER OPIE

THE ANNOTATED BROTHERS GRIMM
MARIA TATAR

SURLALUNE FAIRY TALES
WWW.SURLALUNEFAIRYTALES.COM
HEIDI ANNE HEINER

PUBLIC DOMAIN IMAGES
BROTHERS GRIMM: JERICHAU-BAUMANN (1855)
BLUEBEARD: DORÉ (1862)
GILLES DE RAIS: FROM WIKIMEDIA COMMONS
FITCHER'S BIRD: ARTHUR RACKHAM (1917)

ABOUT THE AUTHOR

Hello! I'm Karly and I'm the person who made this book for you! I hope you enjoyed it. I'm a sculptor, multi-media illustrator and proud humanities nerd. I live in the rural outskirts of Cleveland with my awesome husband Ben (he helped make this book!) and our two dogs, Luna and Stella. They did *not* help make this book, but they frequently sat on me throughout the process.

ABOUT
THE ART

These illustrations are photographs of tiny handmade toys. I sculpted the characters and props with polymer clay, arranged them on sets, then photographed and digitally edited each scene to create the images for this book. This old-school technique is similar to how classic stop motion animation is made. Except here, there's no motion. Or animation. It's all stops.

THE SCHOLARLY
SHOUT-OUTS

Making a book does strange things to one's mind. Throughout the process, I felt like Gollum: A strange creature working alone in the shadows, dreaming of a precious idea and living in a heap of clay, moss, and sticks. It was just as glamorous as it sounds.

A special thanks to **Benjamin West, Pat and Jim Seiple, Emily Savage, Marissa Sertich Velie, Caitlin Shea, Diane Gibbs, Matt and Anna Pawlikowski, Jordan Lee, Christy Ladina, Melissa Clifford, Sue Johansen, and Lisa West Harding** for supporting my crazy ideas, even when I can't quite articulate what I'm making, am covered in moss, or resemble a character from *Lord of the Rings*.

MY PRECIOUS

OH, HEY!

You're still here! If you enjoyed this book, please know that you can make a big difference in a little banana's life by just leaving him a quick review. You know the drill. It takes two minutes. And looks something like this:

And since you're officially Scholarly now (you made it this far), I'd like to cordially invite you to join The Scholarly Fan Club! This way, you'll receive notifications about upcoming banana shenanigans (bananigans?) new issue announcements, and random fun stuff that I only give to people who give me their email address! Join at
thescholarlybanana.com/fanclub

JOIN the SCHOLARLY FAN CLUB

NEXT UP! ISSUE #2:
THE JUNIPER TREE

**ANOTHER LOVELY TALE FROM THE
BROTHERS GRIMM**

www.ingramcontent.com/pod-product-compliance
Lightning Source LLC
Chambersburg PA
CBHW041228070526
44584CB00006B/326